Y0-AGK-271

9/1

FAMOUS LIVES

Marching to Freedom:
The Story of
MARTIN LUTHER KING, JR.

FAMOUS LIVES

Marching to Freedom:
The Story of
MARTIN LUTHER KING, JR.

By Joyce Milton

Gareth Stevens Publishing
MILWAUKEE

For a free color catalog describing Gareth Stevens' list of high-quality books, call 1-800-542-2595 (USA) or 1-800-461-9120 (Canada). Gareth Stevens' Fax: (414) 225-0377.

Library of Congress Cataloging-in-Publication Data

Milton, Joyce.
 Marching to freedom: the story of Martin Luther King, Jr. / by Joyce Milton.
  p. cm. — (Famous lives)
 Rev. ed. of: Marching to freedom. © 1987.
 Includes index.
 ISBN 0-8368-1382-0
 1. King, Martin Luther, Jr., 1929-1968—Juvenile literature.
 2. Afro-Americans—Biography—Juvenile literature. 3. Civil rights workers—United States—Biography—Juvenile literature.
 4. Baptists—United States—Clergy—Biography—Juvenile literature. I. Milton, Joyce. Marching to freedom. II. Title. III. Series: Famous lives (Milwaukee, Wis.).
 E185.97.K5M53 1995
 323'.092—dc20   95-19272
 [B]

The events described in this book are true. The dialogue has been carefully researched and excerpted from authentic biographies, writings, and commentaries. No part of this biography has been fictionalized. To learn more about Martin Luther King, Jr., and the civil rights movement, refer to the list of books and videos at the back of this book or ask your librarian to recommend other fine books and videos.

This edition first published in 1995 by
Gareth Stevens Publishing
1555 North RiverCenter Drive, Suite 201
Milwaukee, Wisconsin 53212, USA

Original © 1987 by Parachute Press, Inc. as a Yearling Biography.
Published by arrangement with Bantam Doubleday Dell Books for Young Readers, a division of Bantam Doubleday Dell Publishing Group, Inc.
Additional end matter © 1995 by Gareth Stevens, Inc.

The trademark Yearling® is registered in the U.S. Patent and Trademark Office.
The trademark Dell® is registered in the U.S. Patent and Trademark Office.

PICTURE CREDITS: Cover: Flip and Debra Schulke/Black Star; AP/Wide World Photos p. 60 (bottom), p. 61 (bottom), p. 63, p. 65 (top); Harry Benson/ Black Star p. 65 (bottom); Bob Fitch/Black Star p. 59 (right); Charles Moore/Black Star p. 59 (top); Flip Schulke/ Black Star p. 59 (bottom left), p. 64 (top); UPI/Bettmann Newsphotos p. 60 (top), p. 61 (top), p. 62, p. 64 (bottom).

Dr. King's speeches are used by permission of Joan Daves. © 1958, 1963 by Martin Luther King, Jr./© 1968 by the estate of Martin Luther King, Jr.

Printed in the United States of America

1 2 3 4 5 6 7 8 9 99 98 97 96 95

Contents

Foreword

IF YOU HAD BEEN A BLACK CHILD GROWING up in the South during the 1930s and 40s, you would have known and hated the name "Jim Crow."

Jim Crow was not a person. The name stood for a system that separated black people from white—a system called segregation.

Every state and city across the South had its own "Jim Crow" laws. These laws told you where you could go to school and where you had to live. They even told you what stores you could shop in. If you and your family went on a trip, you could not stay in the same hotels used by white people. You couldn't eat at the same restaurants, either. If you were really hungry, you might be able to go around to the kitchen door and buy a sandwich to take out.

If you traveled by bus, you had to be careful what section of the bus station you sat in. You would have to remember to use the "colored" restrooms. There were even separate drinking fountains marked "Colored" and "White Only." If you used the wrong one you might get arrested. Once you got on the bus, you would have to sit in the back. And even then, you might have to give up your seat so a white passenger could sit down.

In 1943, a black teenager from Atlanta, Georgia, had an encounter with Jim Crow that he would never forget. The teenager's name was Martin Luther King, Jr. But at the time, no one called him that. In those days, he was known simply as "M.L."

It's the Law

IT SHOULD HAVE BEEN ONE OF THE MOST EX-citing days of his life.

M.L. was only fourteen. But he had been picked ahead of many older students to represent his school at an all-state speech contest in a distant part of the state.

As M.L. got up to give his speech, he could see the smiles on the judges' faces. He knew they were thinking that he looked too young to be in the contest at all. With his short legs and chubby face, M.L. was often mistaken for a grade-school student. But today he was going to try not to let that bother him.

M.L. took a deep breath and began. His voice was deep and powerful. And his speech was full of grown-up ideas. He had worked very hard to make it good. As he talked, he could see the judges begin to sit up straighter in their chairs. He knew they were really listening now, and he was starting to enjoy himself.

When he had finished, M.L. knew he had done well. But he was still surprised when the judges announced their decision. His speech, "The Negro and the Constitution," had won first prize! He had never been so proud.

That evening, M.L. and his speech teacher, Mrs. Bradley, boarded a bus for the trip home to Atlanta. Both of them were feeling tired and happy. They hardly noticed when the bus pulled off the road to make a local stop.

Suddenly, the bus driver started yelling at them. Some new passengers were boarding the bus—white passengers. "Get up, you two," the driver shouted. "The white folks want to sit down."

Mrs. Bradley started to gather her belongings. But she didn't move fast enough to suit the driver. He began to curse. "You black ————. You git up. Now!"

M.L. sat frozen in his seat. No one had ever talked to him that way before.

"Come on now, M.L.," Mrs. Bradley

whispered. "We have to move. It's the law."

He ignored her.

The driver swore at them again. He was so red in the face that he seemed almost ready to explode.

M.L. looked at the driver. Then he looked at Mrs. Bradley. He could see that she was really scared now.

Ever so slowly M.L. stood up.

He had no choice. If he had kept on defying the driver he would have been beaten up or arrested—most likely, both. Mrs. Bradley might have been arrested, too. And he certainly couldn't allow that to happen.

The bus had ninety more miles to go before it reached Atlanta. M.L. and Mrs. Bradley stood in the aisle all the way. The whole time, M.L. kept thinking that his speech had been turned into a bad joke. What was the point of talking about "Negro rights" if you didn't have any?

"That night will never leave my memory," he said years later. "It was the angriest I have ever been in my life."

"You Can't Play Together Anymore"

IN MANY WAYS, M.L. WAS LUCKY. HIS FATHER, the Reverend Martin Luther King, Sr., was the pastor of the Ebenezer Baptist Church. Ebenezer Baptist was one of the largest churches in Atlanta. It had six church choirs! And everyone in town knew Reverend Martin Luther King.

The King family lived in a large, two-story house on a tree-lined street. They were not rich, but they were certainly not poor either. M.L.'s older sister, Chris, took piano lessons. M.L. and his younger brother, Alfred Daniel, nicknamed A.D., went to birthday parties at their friends' nice houses. All the King children had good clothes to wear.

M.L. was born January 15, 1929. And until he was five years old, his life seemed just about perfect. When he went to church, the grownups there made a big fuss over him. The church was like a big, loving family. He spent his days playing with his best friend, the little boy whose father owned the store across the street.

Then came the morning when he and his friend were supposed to start first grade.

M.L. got up early and went to the corner to catch the school bus. But his best friend didn't show up. When he got to school, his friend wasn't in his class either. M.L. worried all day long. After school, he rushed to the front door of his friend's house.

The boy's mother came to the door. "I'm sorry, M.L.," she said. "But you and my son can't play together anymore."

"Why?" he asked.

His friend's mother frowned. "Because we are white and you are colored," she said.

M.L. ran home and told his mother. To his amazement, she said it was true. He and his friend would not be playing together from now on.

That evening at supper, M.L.'s parents tried to explain to him about Jim Crow. Long ago, black people in America had been slaves. Slavery was gone now, but the "Jim

Crow laws" still kept blacks from being first-class citizens. One of those laws said that black children and white children could not go to the same schools.

M.L. thought this was the most unfair thing he had ever heard. If white people were responsible for Jim Crow laws, then they must be mean and hateful. He decided that from then on he was going to hate whites as much as they hated him.

As M.L. grew older, there were times when he could forget all about Jim Crow. As long as he stayed in his neighborhood, where everyone was black like himself, he would have no trouble.

In school, his worst problems were being so short and a preacher's kid, besides. To make up for being a "shrimp," he competed extra hard at everything. On the basketball court, he was the kind of player who hated to pass the ball. He wanted to make every shot himself. Playing football, he charged into the line as if he were in an all-out war. He was so good at his schoolwork that he skipped several grades completely.

M.L.'s parents were always telling him to

take pride in himself. "No one can make you a slave if you don't think like a slave," his father liked to say.

"Don't forget," his mother would add, "you are *somebody*."

But when he left his neighborhood to go downtown, M.L. felt as if the world were telling him that he was worse than a nobody.

One day he would never forget was the day his father took him to buy new shoes for school. He and his dad took seats in the front of the store and waited for someone to help them. They waited a long time, and no one so much as looked their way. Finally, a clerk came over and pointed to the "colored" section in the back of the store.

But Reverend King was too proud to move. "We'll either buy shoes sitting here," he said, "or we won't buy shoes at all."

As soon as he heard that, M.L. knew that he would not be getting any new school shoes that day.

On another day, M.L. was in the car when his father was stopped by a white policeman. "Boy, show me your license," the policeman demanded. Reverend King pointed to M.L., sitting next to him in the front seat. "*That* is a boy," he told the policeman. "I am a *man*. I am the *Reverend* King."

When he was old enough to go downtown alone, M.L. found it impossible to enjoy himself. The first time he went to a movie on his own, he found himself sitting in the balcony, the section of the theater reserved for blacks. His seat was lumpy. The floor was sticky with spilled soda pop and popcorn. Looking over the balcony railing, he could see that the "white" seats downstairs were clean and comfortable. Thinking about those "white" seats ruined the movie for him.

These experiences made M.L. hate whites more than ever. But when he used angry words in front of his father, he just got into trouble. "Love your enemies," Reverend King would tell him. "That's what the Bible says."

M.L. thought this was just about the dumbest thing he had ever heard, even if it was in the Bible. How could you possibly love someone who was your enemy? Why would you even want to?

16

Decisions to Make

B Y THE TIME HE WAS IN HIGH SCHOOL, M.L. was one of the most popular boys in his class. He was a good fast dancer and a sharp dresser. His nickname was "Tweed," after the tweed sports jackets that he liked to wear.

He was also one of the best students in his class. His grades were so good that he was offered a chance to skip his senior year in high school entirely.

So at the age of fifteen, M.L. became a freshman at Morehouse College in Atlanta. Morehouse was an all-black college known for its high academic standards. But M.L. wasn't worried about being too young. He was still living at home, and still seeing his high school buddies—regular guys with nicknames like "Rooster," "Mole," and "Sack." And he had never had any trouble keeping up with his class work.

A few weeks into his first semester at Morehouse, M.L. got a rude shock. His homework was confusing and hard to understand. In class, sometimes he didn't know what the other students were talking about. One of his teachers arranged for him to take an achievement test. It showed that he was four years behind in reading.

At first, M.L. was sure that there had been a mistake. How could he be so far behind when his grades in high school had been so high?

Then one of his professors told him the hard truth. The standards at his old public school had been low. Because the students were all black, the school board hadn't thought it was important for them to have a first-rate education.

M.L. felt cheated. He was so bitter that he even thought about giving up. But his parents refused to let him do that.

Reverend Martin Luther King had great faith in education. When he was a boy, his own parents had been very poor. To earn money, he had stayed home from school to pick cotton and take care of the family mule.

And on the days he was able to go to school, the other children had made fun of him. "Here comes the fool! He smells just like a mule!" they had shouted.

"I may smell like a mule, but at least I don't think like one," he had shouted back.

Reverend Martin Luther King never forgot those taunts. He studied on his own and put himself through high school. Then he put himself through college when he was already a grown man. Now he was determined that his son would not give up on education.

M.L. listened to his dad's advice. He began doing extra work to raise his reading level.

One of his teachers told him about a way to improve his vocabulary. "Look up difficult words in the dictionary, and then practice using them every day," the teacher suggested.

M.L. enjoyed the game so much that his speech was soon filled with unfamiliar words. He never said he was just plain thinking; he was *cogitating*. He was never resting, he was *quiescent*. He especially enjoyed making up new words. When someone

19

asked him if he was an introvert or an extrovert, M.L. said he was an *ambivert*—a little bit of both.

Some of M.L.'s classmates laughed at him. They said he was just a little kid using hard words to make himself feel big. To some extent this may have been true. But M.L. was also saying something very important about himself: He took himself seriously, and he expected the world to take him seriously, too.

Soon he was getting A's again. By his sophomore year he had caught up with his class and was a member of the football team, too.

Another sign that he was growing up was that he was no longer called "Tweed." His family and some of his friends still used the nickname M.L. But more and more he was known as Martin.

Martin had taken his father's advice about staying in school. But it sometimes seemed as if this was the only subject they could agree on.

Reverend King had always wanted his oldest son to become a minister. M.L. had other ideas. He felt that he had already spent enough time in church to last a lifetime. He even wondered whether he was a true Christian, even though he had been baptized.

The Baptist church did not believe in baptizing babies right after they were born. Baptists were expected to make their own decisions to come forward and be baptized. Martin would never forget the day of his baptism, when he was just five years old.

His older sister, Chris, had told her family that she was going to be baptized that Sunday. At the end of the service, when the time came, she left her seat and started down the aisle. Martin jumped out of his seat and trailed along right behind her. He just couldn't stand to let his big sister get ahead of him in anything.

Years later, it occurred to him that this wasn't a very good reason for being baptized. He sometimes wondered if he were in the church only because of his family. He didn't dare mention these doubts at home. But when he started college, he told his parents that he wanted to be a lawyer or doctor. His father was very disappointed.

Then, during his sophomore year, he started to change his mind.

M.L. was the kind of student who drove his teachers crazy by always asking "why?" But it had never occurred to him that it was possible to ask "why" when it came to religion. At home, there could only be one answer to that question: "Because the Bible says so."

At Morehouse, Martin had to take a course in religion. To his surprise, it soon became his favorite subject. His teacher showed him that there were different ways of thinking about God. There was room in the church for people who couldn't help asking "why?"

Martin started to think that he might like to become a Baptist preacher after all. It wasn't easy to tell his dad that he had changed his mind. Finally, though, he managed to break the news.

Secretly, Reverend King was delighted. This was exactly what he had been hoping for all along. But he wanted to make sure that this time his son really knew what he wanted. He told Martin that he would have to prove himself by giving a trial sermon.

His father promised that the test would be easy. The sermon would be scheduled for a small room in the church basement. Only a few people, mostly friends and family, would bother to come.

This sounded all right to Martin.

Of course, word of the event got out. Everyone was curious to hear how the Reverend Martin Luther King's seventeen-year-old son was going to perform. On the day of the sermon, Martin sat stiffly at the front of the small room and watched the rows of folding chairs fill up with people. The older ladies of the church, who still thought of him as Reverend Martin Luther King's little boy, had all shown up. So had many of his friends from high school. And his old girl friends. And his girl friends' families . . .

There were many more people than chairs. And still the crowd kept coming. Martin tried to start the sermon. After a few minutes he had to give up. People were crowded around the door, trying to get in. The service had to be moved upstairs to the main auditorium of the church.

Martin was very nervous, but somehow he managed not to show it. He kept his voice under control. When he finished, everyone said he had passed the test with flying colors.

Later that same year, Martin was ordained as a minister. Ebenezer Baptist, his father's church, voted to hire him as their assistant pastor.

Martin graduated from Morehouse in 1948. At the time, he was dating a girl from one of the wealthiest black families in Atlanta. Reverend King thought his son should get married and stay on at Ebenezer Baptist. The two of them could be a father and son team—pastor and assistant pastor.

Martin was only nineteen and in no hurry to get married. He wanted to go on to study theology. He told his parents that he wanted to go to a school up North—the Crozer Theological Seminary in Chester, Pennsylvania.

"You're mighty young to be going to Crozer," the Reverend Martin Luther King said.

Martin pointed out that if he was old enough to be an ordained minister, he was surely old enough to go to Pennsylvania by himself. His father could not argue with this logic. He gave Martin his blessing.

Going North

MARTIN AND HIS BROTHER, A.D., HAD AL-ways worked at outdoor jobs during their summer vacations. Usually, the jobs were in Atlanta. But one summer before Martin finished college, he and A.D. went North. They found work picking tobacco at a farm in the Connecticut River Valley near Hartford.

Picking tobacco was hard, but Martin and A.D. loved Connecticut. They liked walking down the street, knowing that they could stop at any diner or coffee shop for a hamburger. They didn't have to worry that they would end up in jail for breaking some Jim Crow law. For the first time in their lives they felt really free!

Of course, there was plenty of racial prejudice in Hartford. But Martin and A.D. hardly noticed. Compared to Georgia, Connecticut seemed wonderful to them.

When the summer ended, Martin and

A.D. sadly boarded the train for the trip home. Shortly after the train entered Virginia, they went to the dining car for lunch.

Martin and A.D. sat down at the first empty table they saw. At first they wondered why no one came to serve them. Then a waiter came over and whispered, "I'm sorry, but you can't sit here."

The brothers had forgotten that Jim Crow laws were in effect again as soon as the train entered the South.

Martin and A.D. were led to a table in the rear of the dining car. But that wasn't the end of it. Next, the waiter pulled a curtain around their table so that the white diners couldn't see them.

As Martin later said, it was "as if the curtain had been dropped on my selfhood."

Now that he had finished college, Martin wanted to go back up North. That was his reason for choosing Crozer. Leaving the South would be like stepping out from behind that curtain again, once and for all. He hoped that at Crozer he would be able to forget about segregation and just be himself.

At first, it didn't work out that way.

Crozer was a small school. When Martin arrived in the fall of 1948, there were only one hundred and six students in all—one hundred whites and six blacks.

By now, Martin no longer felt that he hated white people. He had decided that the Jim Crow system was to blame, not people themselves. Still, he wasn't used to being the only black student in many of his classes.

Martin began to feel as if he were onstage 24 hours a day. He knew that many whites thought blacks were lazy and not very clean, so he bent over backward to prove those stereotypes untrue. He was so worried about being late that he would show up half an hour early. He wore a suit and tie every day. His room was spotless. He hardly ever cracked a smile.

Many of Martin's classmates wanted to be friendly. They just didn't know how to talk to someone who seemed so serious all the time. But there were a few white students who were just looking for a chance to cause trouble for Martin. One young man from North Carolina was the worst of all.

Like many schools, Crozer had its share of practical jokers. A favorite trick was to sneak into a freshman's room and pull a "room raid." The jokers didn't do any serious damage. But by the time they were finished the room looked as if a tornado had passed through it.

The student from North Carolina was not very popular. So before long, he became a victim of a "room raid." One evening he came back to the dorm to find his room in a mess. It didn't occur to him that he had been the victim of a prank. He blamed Martin.

Martin was studying alone in his room. Suddenly the North Carolina student came running in. "You can't get away with this!" he shouted.

The next thing Martin knew, the student was waving a gun in his face. "Now I'm going to kill myself a darkie," he threatened.

Martin managed to stay calm. He knew about the room raid. But this was not a good time to try to tell the student that he had been the victim of a joke.

Luckily, three other students heard the shouting. While Martin kept talking, they sneaked into the room and grabbed the student's arm. Then they wrestled him to the floor and took the gun.

The students who had come to help Martin were very upset. They reported the attack to the student council. They were sure that the student would be told to pack his bags and go home.

But Martin would not press charges. The student had come to him and apologized, and Martin had accepted.

At first, the other students thought Martin was wrong. They couldn't understand why he didn't want revenge. But as the days went by, they began to admire him for being big enough to forgive his attacker. The incident made Martin many new friends.

Even the southerner had to admit that he had changed his mind about blacks belonging at Crozer. After all, he was the one who had made a fool of himself, while Martin had stayed cool from first to last.

At about this time Martin was doing a lot of reading about a problem that had bothered him ever since he was a child: Where did evil come from? And how could good people fight evil without becoming evil themselves?

He began to study the life and teachings of Mahatma Gandhi. Gandhi had believed that love and truth were the most powerful forces in the world—so strong that they could defeat an army equipped with guns.

It sounded impractical. But Gandhi had put his ideas to the test and proved them right. He and his followers had used peaceful marches and protests to win India's freedom from British rule.

Martin was not sure that he could ever accept Gandhi's beliefs completely. He still thought there were times when it might be necessary for people to fight back. But reading about Gandhi's life helped him to understand the Bible verse that his father had quoted to him so many times: "Love your enemies."

He had always thought that this was advice meant for the weak and helpless. Now, he saw that he had been wrong. Fighting evil with love had worked for Gandhi in India. He began to wonder whether the same methods could be used to fight injustice in the United States.

Coretta

MARTIN GRADUATED FIRST IN HIS CLASS
at Crozer. His reward was a scholar-
ship for further graduate study. He chose to
go to another northern school, Boston University.

By this time, the Reverend Martin Luther
King, Sr., had forgotten that he had ever
been against Martin's plan to continue his
education. The Kings showed their pride in
Martin by giving him a new car as a gradua-
tion present—a green Chevrolet.

Driving his shiny new car, Martin left for
Boston. He found an off-campus apartment,
which he shared with a friend from Atlanta.

Martin liked Boston, but he was often
lonely. He missed his family. He was even
starting to get homesick for the South, especially for southern cooking.

Neither Martin nor his roommate knew
how to cook. When they wanted a really
good meal they went out to a soul-food res-

taurant called the Western Lunch Box.

One day at the restaurant, Martin got into a conversation with Mary Powell, a woman who was also from Atlanta.

"I wish I knew a few girls from down home," Martin happened to say.

Mrs. Powell thought her friend Coretta Scott might be just right for Martin. Coretta Scott came from Alabama, where her family owned a small trucking company. Like Martin, Coretta loved music. She was studying to become a singer at the New England Conservatory of Music.

Most important, the Scott family, like the Kings, had a tradition of speaking out against segregation. Coretta had made up her mind while she was still in college that she could never love any man who was not ready to fight for justice for black people.

"There's only one problem," Mary Powell warned Martin. "Coretta doesn't go to church very often."

"That's all right," said Martin. And he took down Coretta Scott's phone number.

Martin called Coretta that evening to ask her for a date.

Coretta almost said no. She wasn't sure that she wanted to go out with a preacher. As a favor to Mary Powell, she agreed to have lunch with Martin the next day.

Martin liked Coretta Scott at first sight. She had lovely eyes and a quiet manner. When he started to talk about his studies, Coretta joined right in. Most of the girls he dated did not share his interest in philosophy and politics. He was very impressed to find one who did.

Even before the lunch was finished, Martin had made up his mind. "You have everything I've been looking for in a wife," he blurted out.

Coretta could hardly believe her ears! It was only their first date, and Martin was practically proposing to her.

At first she didn't even think of saying yes. For one thing, she was not sure she would like being a minister's wife. Being married to a preacher was like having a full-time, non-paying job. If she married Martin, it would mean giving up her dream of being a concert singer.

Martin was not one to lose heart easily.

He told Coretta she would change her mind about him—and about being a minister's wife, too. And eventually, she did. The longer she knew Martin, the more she saw that he had the one quality she had always thought was most important of all—he was a fighter.

Coretta Scott and Martin Luther King, Jr., were married in the summer of 1953. A year later, Martin finished the last of his classes in Boston. It was time for him to find a job.

Martin had several offers to become a college teacher. He was tempted to accept one of them. He was never happier than when he was studying and writing. And he and Coretta both knew they would like living on a college campus.

Another invitation had come from the Dexter Avenue Baptist Church in Montgomery, Alabama.

That spring, the Kings went to Montgomery to meet the congregation. And when Sunday morning came, Martin preached a trial sermon.

Martin still looked years younger than his

age. When he appeared in the pulpit, some churchgoers could hardly believe he was old enough to be a minister. "Why, he looks as if he should be home with his mama!" one woman exclaimed.

But the congregation liked what they heard. Martin spoke in a deep, imposing voice. He knew how to fill his sermons with quotations from the great philosophers. Yet he was sincere and friendly, too.

Dexter Avenue had always been a quiet sort of church. The congregation decided it would be nice to have such a thoughtful young man to listen to on Sunday mornings. They invited him to become their permanent pastor.

The Kings now faced a hard choice. Neither Martin nor Coretta really wanted to live in the South again. Both of them hated segregation. They felt lucky to have escaped to the North.

Still, the South was their first home. And Martin had studied many years to be a preacher. He felt he had a duty to go where he was needed most.

It was a hard decision. But the Kings finally told the church that they were willing to come.

The Kings' first year in Montgomery was a busy one.

Martin still had to finish the long paper that was required for his doctoral degree—the highest degree in education. He got up at 5:30 every morning to work on it. The rest of his day was filled with church duties.

Mrs. King had a full schedule, too. She sang in the choir and went to church meetings.

They weren't sorry that they had come back to the South. There was a new spirit in the air, a spirit of change.

In May, 1954, just weeks after they decided to come to Montgomery, the Supreme Court made an important decision. The Court ruled that segregated schools were illegal. Many people thought this meant the beginning of the end of the Jim Crow laws.

Some white politicians vowed to defy the Court. One even boasted that he could stall for a hundred years! But blacks in the South were hopeful. At long last, the government in Washington seemed ready to take up their cause.

The Kings shared these hopes. At the moment, though, they were busy at home. In June, 1955, Martin received his doctoral degree. He became Dr. King. And that fall, Yolanda King, known as "Yoki," was born. She was the first of the Kings' four children.

Then came December 1, 1955—a day that would change the lives of the King family forever.

Don't Ride the Buses!

ON THURSDAY, DECEMBER 1, A WOMAN named Rosa Parks boarded a bus for home. It was the end of another long day for her. Mrs. Parks had put in a full shift at her job at a Montgomery department store. Then she had stayed downtown to do some early Christmas shopping. Luckily, the bus she caught for the trip home was not crowded. She found a seat in the first row of the "colored" section.

Soon the bus began to fill up. The four rows of seats marked "Reserved for Whites" were completely taken. Other white shoppers were standing in the aisle. The driver shouted for the front row of the "colored" section to stand up. They would have to give up their seats to the whites.

Three of the passengers moved right away. But not Mrs. Parks.

"I'll have to call the police," the driver warned her.

Mrs. Parks sighed. "Go ahead and call them."

The driver did just that. When Mrs. Parks still wouldn't budge, she was hauled off to jail.

Mrs. Parks didn't expect her arrest to be big news to anyone. "I don't know why I did it," she said later. "I was just tired. My feet hurt. There was no plan at all."

But once she found herself in jail, Mrs. Parks decided to fight back. Her first move was to call up Edward Nixon, the head of the local branch of the NAACP—the National Association for the Advancement of Colored People. Mrs. Parks told him that she just didn't think it was right that she had been arrested for sitting down while a white passenger stood. All the passengers paid the same fare—why couldn't they be treated the same? She promised that she was ready to take her case all the way to the Supreme Court, if necessary.

Edward Nixon agreed. The time had come to fight back.

Just after dawn on Friday morning, the phone rang at the King house.

Martin picked up the receiver and heard Edward Nixon's voice. "Martin! It's happened again! One of our people has been arrested."

Nixon had already helped Mrs. Parks get out on bail. Now he had an idea. "We've got to boycott the buses," he told Martin. "We have to make it clear to the white folks that we're not gonna stand for this anymore."

Mrs. Parks' trial was set for Monday morning. Nixon's plan was for all the black citizens of Montgomery to stay off the buses that day. They would show the city that they were on Mrs. Parks' side.

Martin hesitated. They had only three days to get the word out. Could they do it? It was going to be a big challenge. "Okay," he said, "I'm with you."

"That's good," said Nixon, " 'cause I already told people to meet at your church tonight to make plans."

At the meeting that evening, everyone voted to go ahead with the boycott. The next morning, a group of women ran off 40,000 leaflets and went around town passing them out. The leaflets said:

Don't ride the bus to work, to town, to school, or anyplace on Monday, December 5.

On Sunday morning, Dr. King and the other black ministers spread the word in their churches. Other volunteers spent the afternoon on the telephone, urging their neighbors to join the protest.

Martin and Coretta worried all weekend. They knew that most black people in Montgomery did not own cars, so they needed the buses to get to work. How many people would be willing to risk losing their jobs? They decided that the boycott leaders would be lucky if six out of ten black riders stayed home.

At 5:30 A.M. the next morning, the Kings were wide awake. A city bus line ran past their house. Usually, the early-morning buses were crowded with black passengers on their way to work.

Anxiously, they stood by their living room window and waited. When the first bus rumbled past, they couldn't believe their eyes. It was empty. The second bus was empty, too. The third bus had two passengers—but both of them were white.

Martin jumped into the family station wagon. For the next hour, he drove around town checking on the other bus lines. He counted just eight black riders on all the buses he saw.

On a normal day in Montgomery, the buses carried 17,500 black passengers!

The leaders of the boycott were overjoyed. They hadn't dared to dream that the plan would work so well. Martin called it a "miracle."

Later that morning, Martin went down to the courthouse for Rosa Parks' trial. If the judge was smart, Martin thought, he would dismiss the case.

But the judge had no such idea. He found Mrs. Parks guilty and fined her ten dollars. Mrs. Parks' lawyer promised to appeal the case.

Now the boycott leaders had a problem: The boycott had been called for one day only. What was going to happen tomorrow morning? And the day after?

The leaders held a meeting that afternoon. They decided to form a group and call it the Montgomery Improvement Association—the MIA, for short. Their first business would be to elect officers.

A man in the back of the room rose to his feet. "I would like to nominate Dr. King for president," he said.

Martin was taken by surprise. He had expected the group to choose Edward Nixon—or perhaps his friend Reverend Ralph Abernathy, who was Rosa Parks' minister. Martin was new to Montgomery. And he was looking forward to being home with his new baby girl. He wasn't sure that he wanted to take on so much responsibility. "I need some time to think this over," he whispered to Edward Nixon.

"You better think fast," Nixon whispered back.

Nixon was right. There were no more nominations. Before Martin could speak up, the election was over. He had been made president of the MIA by a unanimous vote.

Martin was elected because he was a good speaker. He knew how to talk to all kinds of people: rich and poor, educated and uneducated, black and white. Nixon and others knew that he would be a good leader.

Some people suspected that there was another reason why Martin was chosen. Speaking out against segregation was a dangerous business. Certain racist groups, like the Ku Klux Klan, were determined that the South would never change. If things got too bad, the president of the MIA might well have to leave town. Since the Kings had not lived in Montgomery very long, leaving would not be such a great hardship for them.

Martin knew the risks he was taking. Even his family might be in danger. That night he worried about breaking the news to his wife.

But Coretta was not afraid. "Whatever you do, you have my backing," she told her husband.

Martin's duties as MIA president began that very evening. An open meeting had been called at the Dexter Avenue church. Martin was to be the featured speaker. He knew everyone would expect him to know what to do next.

Shortly before seven o'clock, he left for the church. He almost didn't arrive on time. Several thousand people had turned out for the meeting, so he had to leave his car four blocks from the church and push his way through the crowds. The church had been filled for hours.

What could he say to all these people? Martin wondered. Everyone had such high hopes. He didn't want to let them down. Nervously, he made his way to the front of the church and began to speak.

He began by reminding the crowd that their fight was just beginning. For hundreds of years, he told them, black people had been patient. "But there comes a time," he went on, "that people get tired. We are here this evening to say to those who have mistreated us for so long that we are tired—tired of being segregated and humiliated; tired of being kicked about. . . ."

Next, he called on the protestors to be nonviolent. Violence had been used for years to keep black people from demanding their rights. The MIA would show by its methods that it wanted only justice. "One of the great glories of democracy," he reminded the crowd, "is the right to protest for right."

Near the end of his talk, Martin realized he was quoting the very advice that he had argued about so often with his father: "Love your enemies, bless them that curse you, and pray for them that despitefully use you. In spite of the mistreatment that we have confronted, we must not become bitter and end up hating our white brothers. As Booker T. Washington said, 'Let no man pull you so low as to make you hate him.' "

It was a powerful speech. People kept breaking in to cheer and applaud. By the end some of them were weeping. After listening to Dr. King, they had no doubt that the boycott should continue.

Victory

THE MONTGOMERY BUS BOYCOTT LASTED for 381 days.

In the beginning, no one dreamed that it would go on so long. The MIA did not even start out asking for complete integration. They were willing to have blacks sit in the back of the buses, whites in the front. They simply asked that black riders not be forced to stand up so white riders could sit down. Also, the MIA wanted the bus company to hire some black drivers. It didn't seem fair that black riders had to pay their money to a company that hired only white employees.

The city fathers realized that the MIA was being reasonable. They were ready to start talking. Then the bus company's lawyers got involved. According to the lawyers, the MIA was interfering with the company's right to run its business any way it wanted to.

When the bus company refused to give in,

the boycott leaders knew there would be no quick solution.

One of Martin's first steps was to organize a car pool. People who needed rides gathered every morning in churches and parking lots around town. Volunteers with cars drove them to work. In the afternoon, the volunteers made sure everyone got a ride back home. The car pool took care of thousands of people every day.

Other blacks walked many miles every day rather than take a bus. Some of them even turned down rides. They wanted their white neighbors to see them walking.

One day a car pool driver spotted an old woman trudging along by the side of the road. She looked as if she could hardly go another step. The driver pulled up beside her and stopped. "Jump in, Grandmother," he called out. "You don't have to walk."

The old woman shook her head. "I am not walking for myself," she said. "I am walking for my children and grandchildren."

A few protestors did lose their jobs because of the boycott. But not very many. White employers didn't want their businesses to suffer. And white women who had black maids weren't angry enough to start doing their own housecleaning.

There were many white people in Montgomery who had known all along that segregation was wrong. Some felt guilty. And a few even sent secret contributions to the MIA. But very few had the courage to make themselves unpopular by speaking out. One white woman, a city librarian, did write a letter to the newspaper in support of the boycott. After the letter was published, her friends stopped speaking to her. Strangers insulted her on the streets. Two years later, she committed suicide. Many people said she had been hounded to death, all because of that one letter.

In the meantime, the enemies of the boycott were busy thinking up ways to make life difficult for the MIA's leaders. People who drove for the car pool suddenly found they couldn't get automobile insurance. The Kings' insurance was canceled four different times.

Next, the police started arresting car pool drivers for petty traffic violations. Martin himself was stopped for driving thirty miles an hour in a twenty-five mile per hour zone. Instead of just giving him a traffic ticket, the police took him down to the police station, where he was booked, fingerprinted, and thrown into a cell.

Every morning now, the Kings' mailbox was filled with hate mail. The phone rang at all hours of the day and night. Sometimes when Martin answered, the line would go dead. Sometimes a man with a raspy voice would threaten terrible things.

One night the man warned Martin that he had three days to get out of town. If he refused to leave, the man said, "We gonna blow your brains out and blow up your house."

Martin was afraid. He didn't want to die. He certainly didn't want anything to happen to his family. But he couldn't quit now. He would be letting down thousands of people who had put their faith in him.

A few days later, Martin was attending an evening meeting of the MIA. A man came running in with awful news. The Kings' house had been bombed.

Martin left the meeting and raced home. A crowd had already gathered in the street in front of his house. Many in the crowd were angry with the police for not doing more to protect the King family. One man was talking about going home to get his .38 pistol. "The white folks have pushed us around long enough," he muttered. Martin told the man to keep calm. But as he pushed through the police lines, he was not feeling very calm himself.

He found Coretta in the bedroom, shaken but all right.

She had been sitting in the living room when she heard a loud thud out on the porch. At first, she thought that someone had thrown a brick from a passing car. This had happened before. The Kings were almost getting used to it. But something had made her decide to go into the bedroom to check on the baby.

Seconds later, the bomb exploded. The picture window in the living room shattered. Glass flew everywhere. If Coretta had still been in the room, she could have been badly hurt.

The bombing did not succeed in driving

the Kings out of Montgomery. Martin and Coretta felt that God had saved them from serious harm. They became more determined than ever to stay on and keep fighting.

By now, there was no chance that the city leaders would grant the boycotters' demands. They had announced a "get tough" policy. City officials kept thinking of new excuses to arrest Martin and the other boycott leaders.

In October the authorities came up with the worst threat so far. They asked the courts to declare the boycott car pool a "public nuisance." If the courts agreed to shut down the car pool, it would mean failure for the boycott. The protestors were already tired. They couldn't go on if they didn't have some way to get around town.

The MIA leaders had one slim hope. They had filed a lawsuit of their own in the federal courts saying that segregation on buses was unconstitutional. That case was now before the Supreme Court in Washington. The MIA felt sure it was right. The trouble was, the Supreme Court was already being criticized for its earlier ruling against segregated schools. The Court might decide not to get involved this time.

The city's case against the car pool was set for November 13. Martin went down to the courthouse that day with a heavy heart.

The court proceedings dragged on all morning. Then, just before noon, Martin noticed some commotion in the spectators' section. People were whispering excitedly. Newspaper reporters ran for the phones. The mayor and the prosecutors were called out of the room.

"Something is wrong," Martin told one of his lawyers.

Finally, one of the reporters came up to the defense table and handed Martin a slip of paper. Eagerly Martin read the message: The Supreme Court had just ruled in favor of the MIA. Not only that, but the Court had given the MIA even more than it had asked for back when the boycott started. From then on, there would be no segregated seating on buses, period.

On December 21, 1956, Martin, Mrs. Parks, and Edward Nixon were part of the first integrated group of riders to board a Montgomery bus.

As Martin dropped his fare in the box, the bus driver asked him, "You are Dr. King, aren't you?"

Martin tensed. "Yes I am."

"Well, we are glad to have you this morning," the driver said with a smile.

Martin smiled back and took his seat at the front of the bus. It seemed almost incredible that he had gone through so much for the right to enjoy such a simple, everyday thing as a bus ride.

Not everyone was as ready to accept the situation as that bus driver had been.

There were still a few fanatics who were determined to scare black riders away from the buses. One black woman passenger was shot in the leg. A teenage girl was beaten up by four men at a bus stop. The Reverend Ralph Abernathy, Martin's good friend and Rosa Parks' minister, had both his house and his church bombed in one night.

Even whites who had been against the boycott all along were disgusted. The editor of the pro-segregation newspaper wrote an editorial asking for peace. The city offered a $4,000 reward for information about the crimes. Seven white men were arrested. None of the men were ever convicted, but the violence did stop. Once the troublemakers knew that the majority was turning against them, they gave up.

By spring the city was quiet again. Whites and blacks sat side by side on the buses, just as if they had always done so. As Martin later wrote, integration had come to Montgomery and "the skies did not fall." People all over the country were talking about the "miracle of Montgomery."

We Shall Overcome

MARTIN LUTHER KING, JR.'S, LEADERSHIP of the bus boycott made him a famous man. His picture appeared on the cover of *Time* magazine. Job offers poured in from all over the country. One of them was for the sort of college teaching position that Martin had always dreamed of. If he accepted, he would have time to study and write. There would be time to spend with his family, too.

But black organizations all over the South were hoping to duplicate the miracle of Montgomery. Many of them were turning to Dr. King for help and advice. It was no time to think about taking a quiet job.

So many requests came in that Martin felt overwhelmed. How could he possibly answer them all?

In 1957, Martin invited more than a hundred black leaders to come to Montgomery for a planning session. The group decided to form an organization called the Southern Christian Leadership Conference—the SCLC. Its goal was to help churches and civil rights groups fight against segregation. When it came time to elect officers, the group chose Dr. King by a unanimous vote. His friend Reverend Ralph Abernathy became treasurer.

Martin almost did not get a chance to serve.

He had written a book called *Stride Toward Freedom* that told the story of the boycott. The book was so successful that Martin was invited to come to New York to appear on the *Today* show. While he was in New York, he agreed to sign copies of his book at a department store in Harlem.

Martin was at a table signing books when a well-dressed black woman pushed her way through the crowd that surrounded him. "Are you Martin Luther King?" she asked.

"Yes—" he started to say.

"I've been after you for five years," the woman shouted.

Martin's mouth dropped open in shock. Looking down, he saw that the woman had plunged a sharpened letter opener into his chest. The stabbing happened so fast he hadn't even felt the blade going in.

The letter opener was shaped like a tiny Japanese sword. It looked almost like a toy, but it was a deadly weapon. Martin's first impulse was to reach down and pull the thing out. But he knew that could make the wound worse. He tried to move as little as possible until the ambulance arrived.

Later at the hospital, a doctor told him that he had saved his own life. The blade had been resting against his aorta, the body's largest artery. "You're lucky that you didn't have to sneeze," the doctor said. "If you had, you probably would have bled to death."

Everyone was shocked that Martin Luther King would be attacked in Harlem—and by a black person at that. Even the woman who did the stabbing couldn't explain why she had done it.

Martin asked the police to see that the woman was sent to a hospital instead of to jail. Despite his narrow escape from death, he was more determined than ever to go on working for civil rights. He felt that he had been given a "second chance" at life, and that God must have some special plan for him.

For several years, Martin had two full-time jobs. He was the leader of the SCLC, and he was also the full-time pastor of the Dexter Avenue church.

By 1960, he realized that he would have to make a choice. The King family decided to leave Montgomery and return to Atlanta. There Martin could preach part-time as his father's assistant at Ebenezer Baptist. His new job would give him more time to direct the SCLC freedom movement and travel around the country, speaking against segregation.

The sales of his book, plus income from speeches and articles, were making Martin a fairly rich man. But Martin did not want to spend all his money on himself. He thought that too much luxury made people soft. Rich people had too much to lose. After a while, they no longer wanted to make sacrifices to do God's work.

Martin kept just enough money to support his family. He gave the rest to the SCLC for its work.

The King family never had an expensive car or a big bank account. Yet they never bragged about the sacrifices they were making. Few people had any idea that they were giving away so much.

The Kings moved to Atlanta in January, 1960. It was a discouraging winter for Dr. King and the SCLC. In spite of their hard work, there was almost as much segregation as ever. Sometimes it seemed as if the South would never change.

Then, on February 1, 1960, something dramatic happened. Four black students in Greensboro, North Carolina, walked up to a Woolworth's lunch counter and sat down. They told the waitress that they meant to "sit in" until someone served them.

When the news reached the students' school, others came to join them. Soon college students were organizing sit-ins in other states, too.

While they were "sitting in," the young people often linked arms and sang:

"Oh deep in my heart, I do believe
We shall overcome some day."

And they stayed put until they either got served or got arrested. Usually, they were arrested.

Many people, and some black leaders, were worried about the sit-ins. They thought the students were too impatient. They didn't see how people so young could accomplish anything worthwhile.

But Martin disagreed.

The students looked up to Dr. King as a hero. They asked him for help and advice. And he did not let them down.

When a sit-in started in Atlanta, he decided to take part. He joined 75 students who were sitting in at a snack bar in Rich's department store. The police arrested everyone for trespassing.

The students were all released on bail within three days. Martin was sentenced to four months at hard labor.

He was prepared to serve out his time in jail. What choice did he have? But his friends and family were frightened. They were afraid that he would never get out of prison alive.

In the middle of Martin's first night in

jail, he was shaken awake by one of his guards. "King! Get up!" the man ordered. Then he slapped a pair of handcuffs around Martin's wrists and pushed him out into the hall.

The next thing Martin knew, he was in the back seat of a police car. The car hurtled along through the night at top speed.

"What's going on?" Martin asked. "Where are you taking me?" But the guards refused to tell him anything.

When dawn came, Martin found himself inside the gates of Reidsville, a maximum security prison hundreds of miles from Atlanta. Reidsville had a bad reputation. Some prisoners had been killed or injured in fights. Others had been shot by guards, supposedly for trying to escape. Martin wondered if something similar was going to happen to him.

Help came from an unexpected source. Senator John F. Kennedy was running for president that year. He heard about Dr. King's four-month sentence and thought it was unfair. Robert Kennedy, his brother's campaign manager, phoned the judge to ask him to change his mind.

After two days at Reidsville, Martin was suddenly released. Friends and supporters filled the Ebenezer Baptist Church to celebrate his return home.

Martin was grateful to the Kennedys, but he knew he had not seen his last jail cell.

For years now, some policemen had tried to scare black protestors by throwing them in jail. But the protestors had figured out that the police could never arrest everyone who opposed segregation. They decided to turn the police tactics upside down.

Across the South, civil rights groups started to organize protest marches. The new goal was to go right down to city hall and demand equality. If the marchers got arrested, so much the better. "Fill the jails!" was the motto of the day. Eventually, southern cities would have to accept integration, just to get life back to normal.

Protest marches often worked. But not always.

In 1962 a local group in Albany, Georgia, invited Martin to come march with them. But there would be no miracle in Albany.

At first, it seemed that the march had been successful.

The Albany city council agreed to integrate the bus station. But the next day, the bus company shut down. Later, the city closed the swimming pool rather than let black children swim there. The chairs were removed from the public library so that blacks and whites could not sit and read at the same tables.

Martin kept telling his followers not to be discouraged. If they just kept on marching peacefully for justice, eventually they would win. But in his heart he wondered what was going to happen next.

(left) The Reverend Martin Luther King, Sr., and his son Martin, Jr., attend a civil rights meeting in Atlanta, Georgia.

(above) Martin honors Mahatma Gandhi, a believer in non-violence, by keeping a portrait of him in his office.

(left) The Reverend Martin Luther King, Jr., gives a sermon to his large congregation.

(right) After Rosa
Parks was arrested
for refusing to give
her bus seat to a
white passenger,
the bus boycott
in Montgomery,
Alabama, began.
The incident marked
the beginning
of the civil rights
movement, Decem-
ber 1955.

(above) Martin's mother and his wife Coretta
visit him in the hospital after he was stabbed by
a woman in New York, 1958.

(left) Martin awaits his release from jail after one of his many arrests.

(below) In Birmingham, Alabama, July 1963, "Bull" Connor orders firefighters to spray protestors.

(above) Dr. King delivers his now famous "I Have a Dream" speech in Washington, D.C., August 28, 1963.

(right) In 1964, Martin Luther King, Jr., at age 35, was the youngest man to have ever been awarded the Nobel Peace Prize.

(above) Dr. King and Coretta lead the 1965 five-day march from Selma, Alabama, to the state capital. With them (below) are flute players, flag carriers, and the man who walked the fifty-mile trip on crutches.

(above) Because of his busy schedule, Martin was often on the road. He cherished the times he could spend with his family.

(below) In 1964, President Lyndon B. Johnson shakes Martin's hand and gives him one of the pens used to sign the Civil Rights Act.

(left) Martin Luther King, Jr., stands on the balcony of the Lorraine Motel where he was shot down the following day, April 4, 1968.

(below) Coretta and the Kings' four children (from youngest to oldest), Bernice, Dexter, Marty, and Yolanda, attend Martin's funeral.

The Children's Crusade

"**B**LOOD WILL RUN IN THE STREETS!" PO-lice chief Eugene "Bull" Connor pre-dicted.

Connor had just learned that Martin Luther King's civil rights crusade was com-ing to Birmingham, Alabama. Birmingham was one of the largest cities in the South. It was also one of the most segregated. Bull Connor was going to make it his business to see that it stayed that way.

Dr. King knew that Birmingham would be the biggest challenge of his life. He also had a personal reason for being interested in the city. His brother, Alfred Daniel, lived there. Like Martin, A.D. had become a Bap-tist minister. He was also a leader of the civil rights movement in Birmingham.

Martin and the SCLC arrived in Birming-ham in the spring of 1963. During the first week of marching, more than three hundred people were arrested. Martin and Reverend

Ralph Abernathy went to jail on Good Friday.

Martin spent the Easter holiday in solitary confinement. He and Reverend Ralph Abernathy weren't allowed to talk to each other. For several days, he wasn't even allowed to call home. His family was terribly worried.

Finally, eight days later, Martin and Reverend Ralph Abernathy were released on bail. As soon as he was free, Martin learned that there was a problem. It was getting harder every day to find more people who were willing to get arrested.

Most of the marchers had families to support. As long as they were in jail, they could not work and earn money. And later, when the cases came to trial, they would miss still more work. Some people had struggled all their lives to have houses of their own. Now they had to mortgage them to raise bail money. Other people were told by their bosses that they could be fired for having police records. Even some very brave people were saying that they had to put their families' welfare first.

Some of the younger SCLC workers had

an idea. Why not call on college and high school students? College students had proved their courage before. Maybe the students of Birmingham could help now.

The SCLC put out a leaflet asking students to come to a meeting at a local church. The workers hoped a few dozen students would show up. Instead, nearly a thousand young people answered the call. Many of the volunteers were still in grade school.

The workers tried to turn the grade school students away. But the children hung around the church door, begging to be let in. In the end, only a few six- and seven-year-olds were sent home. Children eight and over were allowed to march.

The children's crusade began on May 2. Almost a thousand children filled the streets and began marching toward the Birmingham city hall. Other children left their classrooms to join them. At one school, the principal locked the gates to keep his pupils inside. The children climbed out windows and over the high gates to join the march.

As they walked, the children sang protest songs like "We Shall Overcome" and "Ain't

Gonna Let Nobody Turn Me Round." Some of them made up songs of their own. One of the favorites was:

> "It ain't nice to block the door,
> It ain't nice to go to jail.
> There are nicer ways to do it,
> But the nice ways always fail."

At first, the police didn't think the children knew what they were doing. One of them stopped an eight-year-old who was marching with her mother. "What do you want, little girl?" he demanded.

The girl looked up into the policeman's eyes. "F'eedom," she lisped. She couldn't pronounce the word quite right, but she knew what it meant.

At once, her answer was echoed by other marchers around her. "FREEDOM! FREEDOM!" they shouted. "WE WANT FREEDOM!"

The child marchers were more disciplined than many adult groups. None of them struck out at the police or yelled angry words. But a few did find nonviolent ways to keep the police busy. Small groups would leave the march and take off through the alleys, leading the police on a wild-goose chase. When the police were completely lost and confused, the children slipped away and rejoined the march.

That first day 959 children were arrested. The police had to call out the school buses to take their young prisoners to jail.

The next morning, twice as many children showed up ready to march. Many more adults came out, too, inspired by the children's example. The demonstration was the biggest Birmingham had seen so far.

The previous day, Bull Connor had not known quite what to do about the children's crusade. But this time, he was prepared to take a tough stand. He had called out the city firefighters. His special corps of trained attack dogs was on hand, too.

The marchers started out bravely, singing to keep their spirits up. Then they turned the corner into a downtown street that led to city hall. A solid wall of police and firemen blocked the way. The police had their billy clubs drawn. German shepherd attack dogs were barking and pulling at their leashes. The firefighters stood silently, their high-pressure hoses aimed at the marchers.

"Let 'em have it!" Bull Connor shouted.
Suddenly, there was pandemonium.

A blast from the fire hoses knocked down the front row of marchers. Then police charged. People trying to get up and run were knocked down and beaten. Then came the dogs, snapping at any leg or arm that got within reach. Some bystanders started throwing rocks and bottles back at the police.

Martin was horrified. He hadn't really believed that Bull Connor would use violence against the children.

Newspaper and TV reporters called what happened that day the "Battle of Birmingham." Photographs of children being bitten by police dogs and beaten with clubs were flashed all over the country.

The protestors wanted to show that they could not be scared into quitting. So two days later, they started another march. This time, when they got to the police lines, they refused to turn back. Instead, they dropped to their knees in prayer. "Turn on your water! Turn loose your dogs!" they called out. "We are here until we die."

Connor answered by giving his usual order: "Let 'em have it!"

But this time, nothing happened. The police and firefighters refused to obey. Some of them had tears in their eyes.

It took the marchers a while to realize that no one was going to try to stop them. Then, a few at a time, they rose to their feet and passed through the police lines.

A few days later, the city agreed to many of the marchers' demands. There would be no more segregation in Birmingham stores and restaurants. And these businesses also promised to start hiring black workers.

This was by no means the end of trouble in Birmingham. A day after the agreement was signed, A.D. King's home was blown up by a time bomb. And months later, another bomb exploded in a Birmingham Sunday School, killing four little girls.

Even though the violence continued, the children's crusade was a turning point in the struggle for civil rights. Many white Americans had never given much thought to what it would be like to be black and live under segregation. But the pictures they saw on TV touched their hearts. If children got beaten up just for wanting freedom, then something must be terribly wrong.

"I Have a Dream"

THE SUMMER OF 1963 WAS A SEASON OF marches. Inspired by Dr. King and the children of Birmingham, black Americans all over the country began marching for freedom. In more than 250 southern cities and towns, the Jim Crow laws were abolished. In the North, black groups organized to demand equality in jobs and housing.

In the meantime, Dr. King and other civil rights leaders were planning the biggest march of all—a march on the nation's capital.

The idea of a gigantic march on Washington, D.C., had been around for a long time. Now it was an idea whose time had come.

President Kennedy had watched the TV reports from Birmingham along with the rest of America. A month later, he announced that he was sending Congress a new civil rights bill. If the bill passed, it would no longer be legal for stores, restaurants, and hotels to refuse to serve black customers.

Black leaders wanted to make sure that Congress would do what the President asked. They hoped for a big turn-out for the march that would show their support for the bill.

On the morning of August 28, marchers from all over the country began to pour into Washington. There were young marchers and old, blacks and whites, too. There were hundreds of thousands of people—so many that no one could count them.

The great crowd swelled through the streets. Everyone was headed for the Lincoln Memorial, where a huge rally was already starting.

Dozens of celebrities were on hand to greet the crowd. Jackie Robinson, the first black major league baseball player was there. . . . So were singers Harry Belafonte and Lena Horne and Sammy Davis, Jr. . . . So was the folksinger Odetta and the great gospel singer Mahalia Jackson. White stars had also come to lend their support: Bob Dylan, actors Charlton Heston and Burt Lancaster. And many more. There were politicians, too. And church leaders. All of them wanted a chance to speak to the crowd.

By the time Martin Luther King, Jr., was introduced, the rally had been going on for more than two hours. It was a hot summer day. The marchers had been in the sun a long time. People were getting thirsty and restless. Some were getting ready to leave.

Martin stood in front of the microphone and looked out at the vast crowd. He had been told he could talk for just eight minutes. What could he say in eight minutes that would make a difference?

He started by reading the speech he had prepared. He reminded the crowd that it was one hundred years since President Lincoln freed the slaves. And still, black Americans were not really free. In the South, many blacks still did not have the right to vote. In the North, many saw "nothing worth voting *for.*"

As he spoke, Martin could see that the crowd was beginning to pay close attention. He himself felt caught up in the emotion of the moment.

Setting his notes aside, he began talking about his vision of America's future.

"I have a dream," he said, "that one day

. . . the sons of former slaves and the sons of former slaveowners will be able to sit down together at the table of brotherhood. . . .

"I have a dream that my four little children will one day live in a nation where they will not be judged by the color of their skin but by the content of their character.

"I have a dream today."

Now the crowd was totally caught up by the sweeping flow of the words. People who had been getting ready to leave sat down again. Whole sections of the audience started swaying back and forth, clapping their hands softly.

In ringing phrases, Martin conjured up his dream of an America united. "Let freedom ring from every hill . . ." he said. "From every mountain top, let freedom ring.

". . . we are speeding up that day when all of God's children, black men and white men, Jews and Gentiles, Protestants and Catholics, will be able to join hands and sing in the words of the old Negro spiritual: 'Free at last! Free at last! Thank God Almighty, we are free at last!' "

Those who heard Martin Luther King's

speech that day would never forget the experience. The dream was no longer his alone. It had become part of the American dream, a dream that belonged to everyone.

Americans soon needed to draw on the hope that Dr. King gave them that day. Three months later, on November 22, President Kennedy was assassinated. It was a terrible time for the country.

When Kennedy died, his civil rights bill was still in the Congress. No one knew what would become of it.

The new president was Lyndon Johnson. In one of his first speeches after taking office, Johnson asked Congress to pass the civil rights bill. He said it would make a wonderful memorial to President Kennedy. Ashamed of all its delays, Congress passed the bill. It was signed into law in July, 1964.

We Have Overcome

D R. KING WAS NOW 35 YEARS OLD. HE WAS already one of the most famous men in the world. *Time* magazine chose him as its Man of the Year for 1963. Ten months later, he received a much greater honor, the Nobel Peace Prize. This international award, sponsored by the Nobel Foundation in Oslo, Norway, is given to those who have made major contributions toward promoting peace. Dr. King was the youngest person ever to receive the award.

Perhaps more important, he was the leader that black Americans admired and trusted above all others.

But it wasn't easy being the man in the spotlight.

Martin gave hundreds of speeches every year. He had been arrested 13 times. He was always on the go. In 1963 alone, he traveled more than 275,000 miles.

The Kings had four children by now, but they seldom got the chance to see their father for more than a day or two at a time. It bothered Martin that he was hardly ever at home with his family.

There was a story he liked to tell about his daughter Yoki. When Yoki was a toddler she wanted to go to Fun City, an amusement park in Atlanta. Martin had to explain to her that she would not be allowed in. Fun City was for whites only.

Not long after, Martin was arrested. Mrs. King wondered how she could explain the reasons to her little girl. Finally she told her, "Your daddy is in jail because he is fighting against segregation."

Yoki took the news calmly. "Tell him to stay there until I can go to Fun City," she said.

The story was funny. But it was sad, too. After a while, the King children began getting used to hearing that their father was in jail yet again.

After he won the Nobel Peace Prize, Dr. King was in more demand than ever. He marched and preached in many different cities. But his longest and most important campaign was in Selma, Alabama.

The trouble in Selma started because a group of black citizens tried to register to vote.

For many years, very few black people had voted in the South. Some states put a tax on voting to scare poor blacks away. Some made new voters pass a reading test. The test for whites was easy. The test for blacks could be impossible to pass. Blacks who wanted to vote were sometimes asked to read and explain pages from law books. They were asked questions that would stump many lawyers.

Many blacks were simply afraid. It took a lot of courage to walk into the courthouse and demand to register to vote. The new civil rights law was supposed to protect the voting rights of every citizen. But students who came to Selma to urge black people to register found that the law was not working there. The students were threatened. A few whites vowed to shoot blacks who tried to vote.

Martin arrived in Selma early in 1965. Compared to Birmingham, Selma was a small, sleepy country town. It looked so peaceful. But marchers met more violence there than they had ever seen in downtown Birmingham. Police chased some marchers with electric cattle prods. Many other marchers were beaten up.

One teenage boy was beaten so badly that he died. A few days later, a white minister was ambushed on the street and killed.

Martin decided to lead a march all the way to Montgomery, the state capital. This was a very dangerous plan. Marchers on lonely country roads would make easy targets. Alabama's governor George Wallace made a speech saying he could not promise to protect the march. This was too much for President Johnson. He called out the National Guard.

Despite the danger, several thousand people took part in the march. Hundreds walked the entire fifty miles from Selma to Montgomery. In some places, armed soldiers lined the roads as the marchers passed by. Even so, a group that called itself the "Confederate Air Force" flew overhead, "bombing" the line of march with insulting leaflets.

After five days, the marchers reached Montgomery. They were led by a young man dressed as "the Spirit of 76" who played "Yankee Doodle" on a flute. Beside him was a marcher who had only one leg— he had walked the fifty miles on crutches!

Governor Wallace refused to come out of his office to meet the marchers. Still, they knew they had won a victory. The entire country had watched the marchers' progress on the nightly TV news shows. And President Johnson had already drafted a bill that would give more protection to blacks who wanted to vote.

As the marchers entered Montgomery they changed the words of their favorite anthem. Instead of "we *shall* overcome" they sang "we *have* overcome." Ten years after the Montgomery bus boycott began, Martin had returned to the city in triumph.

Where Do We Go From Here?

WHERE DO WE GO FROM HERE?
This was the title of Dr. King's latest book. It was also a question that he was asking himself.

America seemed to be sinking into a swamp of violence. In spite of his victorious march through Alabama, more civil rights workers were killed there. Riots were breaking out in the poor black neighborhoods of cities all over the country. Some of the younger black leaders no longer even talked about peaceful integration. They were saying that the time had come to fight back.

America was also sending soldiers to fight a war in Vietnam. Martin thought this was a terrible mistake. Early in 1967, he started speaking out against the war.

These speeches made some of Martin's oldest friends angry. Didn't he have enough to do fighting for civil rights at home? Most

Americans approved of the war. Martin would only make trouble for himself, and maybe for all blacks, with his unpopular ideas.

But he refused to listen. All his life he had hated war and killing. "I can't be silent," he told his friends. "I am a citizen of the world."

Martin was also worrying more and more about the problems of black people who lived in the North. For many years, black people in the North had enjoyed freedoms that southern blacks could only dream about. But they still did not have equality. Many had no jobs. Many lived crowded together in slums.

Martin decided that he wanted to learn firsthand about race problems in the North. In 1966 the entire King family moved into an apartment in a Chicago housing project.

It did not take them long to start learning. The apartment was crowded. The streets were dangerous. Mrs. King and the children were afraid to go out at night. But when the whole family stayed home, they got on one another's nerves. They had never argued so much before.

At the time, many young civil rights leaders were using the slogan "Black Power." Martin was not against the idea of Black Power. But he thought that "Poor People's Power" would be a better motto. He had always tried to find ways to call on the highest ideals of people of all races. And one thing he had learned in Chicago was the poor people of all races have similar problems.

When civil rights groups marched on Washington, they had forced Congress to pay attention to them. Why couldn't poor people band together and ask Congress for help?

Martin began to organize a Poor People's March. Caravans of the poor—white and black—would start out from cities all over the country. Once again, the great march would end in Washington. This time, however, the marchers wouldn't leave after a few speeches. They would stay around. Maybe they could even camp in tents in the city parks.

Planning for the campaign went slowly. The march would cost a lot of money. And many of Martin's oldest supporters were not sure that the march would succeed. President Johnson was angry with Dr. King for his speeches against the war. This time, the marchers would not be able to count on any help at all from the White House.

Other leaders had simply lost faith in the power of nonviolence. And in Dr. King, too. He knew that behind his back some people had a new nickname for him: Martin Loser King. In the past, he had been called a miracle worker. Now, he was under pressure to work miracles all the time. Anything less and some people were disappointed.

Still, he refused to give up. When others grew discouraged, he worked twice as hard. He began crisscrossing the country, trying to get money and volunteers for the caravan.

One of the cities he visited was Memphis, Tennessee.

The sanitation workers in Memphis were on strike. Nine out of ten of the workers were black. All of them were underpaid. Martin thought the strike was a perfect example of poor people getting together to fight for a better life. He agreed to lead the strikers on a march through the city.

The Memphis march began like many

others. Martin was in the lead. Behind him, hundreds of strikers filled the streets.

Suddenly, there came the sound of breaking glass. Then shouts and running feet. On the fringes of the crowd, some teenagers were throwing stones into store windows. When the police tried to arrest the youths, they fought back.

Soon all of downtown Memphis was in an uproar. Eighty people were hurt in the fighting. Stores were looted. Cars set on fire. One black teenager was shot and killed.

Many people said that Memphis was the end of the road for nonviolence. The movement was finished.

But Martin refused to accept defeat.

The next day, he learned that the trouble had not been caused by the strikers. A teenage gang called the Invaders had been saying that breaking windows and looting was the best way for poor blacks to get attention. It was their wild talk that had set off the fighting.

Martin arranged a meeting with the Invaders. He tried to tell them that just being angry wasn't enough. When a riot started, it was almost always the poorest people who got hurt. Even getting into the newspapers and on TV wasn't enough. It was important to have a long-range plan.

The Invaders were young and impatient. They weren't convinced by Martin's logic. But they were impressed that the famous Dr. Martin Luther King was willing to take the time to argue with them. They promised to give him a chance to do things his way. The next time he marched, they would see that there was no trouble.

Another march was set for Friday, April 5. Martin arrived in Memphis two days early, on Wednesday afternoon.

That night he gave a speech at the Masonic Temple in downtown Memphis. For some reason, he started to talk about the time he had been stabbed in Harlem. He had been so close to death. If he had died then, he would have missed seeing the miracle of Birmingham. He would have missed the march on Washington.

There were still difficult days ahead, he told the crowd. He wasn't sure that God would let him live to see the final victory.

But, he said, "It really doesn't matter with me now. Because I've been to the mountain top. . . . I've *seen* the Promised Land. And I may not get there with you. But I want you to know tonight that we as a people *will* get to the Promised Land. So I'm happy tonight. I'm not worried about anything."

Some of Martin's friends were frightened. They had heard their leader speak about dying before. But this time, he sounded as if death were very close. It was almost as if he could see into the future.

Martin was staying at the Lorraine Motel in Memphis. The Lorraine was not the fanciest hotel in town, but it had a black owner. And Martin liked to help out black businessmen whenever he could.

Other SCLC staff members had also checked into the Lorraine. Reverend Ralph Abernathy, Martin's friend and partner since the days of the Montgomery bus boycott, was there. So were some of Martin's younger aides, Reverend Andrew Young of Atlanta and Reverend Jesse Jackson.

Thursday was a busy day for all of them. They spent hours planning for the march.

They also made a trip to the courthouse to convince a city judge that this time there would be no trouble.

By dinnertime, everyone was tired and hungry. The whole group had been invited to dinner at the home of a local minister and his wife.

At six o'clock everyone was dressed and ready to go. The minister and his wife went down to the parking lot. The other staff members were already gathered there.

"Just a minute," said Reverend Ralph Abernathy. "Let me put on some after-shave."

Martin stepped out onto the balcony to wait.

A few seconds later, Reverend Ralph Abernathy heard a popping sound. He saw his friend stagger backward and sink to the balcony floor. Abernathy bent over Martin, trying to protect and comfort him.

Someone called an ambulance. But there was nothing the doctors could do. Martin had been shot in the head. He died in the hospital an hour later.

The news that Martin Luther King, Jr.,

had been murdered caused an explosion of anger and frustration. There were riots in more than a hundred cities.

The hunt for Dr. King's killer dragged on for days. Finally, a white man named James Earl Ray was arrested. Ray was a drifter who had been in trouble with the law for most of his life. He was eventually convicted of murder.

Many people thought that the murder of Dr. King had cost him more than his life. The hatred and violence that he fought so hard to end had triumphed.

But Martin Luther King's message was not to be forgotten.

On the day of his funeral, the streets of Atlanta were filled with mourners. Fifty thousand people marched behind the hearse that took Dr. King's body to its last resting place.

And in 1985, Congress voted to establish a federal holiday in Dr. King's honor. Only three other individuals have ever been honored in this way: Christopher Columbus is remembered on Columbus day. And the birthdays of Presidents George Washington and Abraham Lincoln are celebrated together on Presidents' Day.

Martin Luther King Day was celebrated across the nation for the first time in 1986. Many speakers on that day recalled a quotation from the Old Testament story of Joseph and his brothers:

"Here comes this dreamer. Come now, let us kill him . . . and we shall see what will become of his dreams."

Now Martin Luther King, Jr., belonged to history. It will be up to new generations to say what will become of his dreams of freedom and equality for all.

Highlights in the Life of
MARTIN LUTHER KING, JR.

1929   Martin is born on January 15 in Atlanta, Georgia, where his father is the pastor of Ebenezer Baptist Church.

1944   Martin enrolls as a freshman at Morehouse College in Atlanta, an all-black college known for high academic standards, when he is only fifteen years old.

1946   At the age of seventeen, Martin delivers his first sermon in his father's church. He is ordained as a minister later that year and hired as assistant pastor.

1948   Martin graduates from Morehouse College at age nineteen. He enrolls at Crozer Theological Seminary in Pennsylvania, where he later graduates first in his class.

1953   Martin and Coretta Scott are married. Martin had met Coretta while he was a graduate student at Boston University and she was a student at the New England Conservatory of Music.

1954   Martin becomes pastor of the Dexter Avenue Baptist Church in Montgomery, Alabama. The same year, the Supreme Court rules that segregated schools are illegal.

1955   Martin receives his doctoral degree from Boston University. Martin and Coretta's first child, Yolanda, is born in the fall.

Rosa Parks, a black woman, is arrested in December for refusing to give up her seat to a white passenger on a Montgomery bus. Martin helps organize a boycott of city buses. He is elected president of the Montgomery Improvement Association and begins actively advocating non-violent protest. This time is considered by many to be the beginning of the Civil Rights Movement in the United States.

The Kings's house is bombed. Coretta and baby Yolanda, who are home at the time, are unharmed.

1956   Martin, Rosa Parks, and Edward Nixon join others on December 21 as the first integrated group of riders on Montgomery buses.

1957   Martin organizes the Southern Christian Leadership Conference (SCLC) to help churches and civil rights groups fight segregation.

1958   While signing books at a New York City department store, Martin is stabbed. He is hospitalized but is not seriously injured.

1960   Martin and Coretta move from Montgomery to Atlanta, where Martin becomes his father's assistant at Ebenezer Baptist Church. In addition, he continues to direct the SCLC and give speeches throughout the United States.

Martin is arrested for trespassing while supporting students at a sit-in. He is sentenced to four months of hard labor but released several days later after intervention from John and Robert Kennedy.

1963   Martin delivers his famous "I Have a Dream" speech in Washington, D.C., on August 28.

1964   The Civil Rights Act is signed, prohibiting racial discrimination in public places and requiring equal opportunity in employment and education. Martin is awarded the Nobel Peace Prize at the age of 35, the youngest person ever to win this honor.

1965   Martin leads the five-day civil rights march from Selma to Montgomery, Alabama.

1968   On April 4, Martin is shot and killed by James Earl Ray in Memphis, Tennessee. He dies at the age of thirty-nine.

For Further Study

More Books to Read

I Have a Dream: The Story of Martin Luther King. Margaret Davidson (Scholastic)

The Life and Death of Martin Luther King, Jr. James Haskins (Lothrop, Lee and Shepard)

The Life and Words of Martin Luther King, Jr. Ira Peck (Scholastic)

Martin Luther King Day. Linda Lowery (Carolrhoda)

Martin Luther King, Jr. Margaret Jones (Childrens Press)

Martin Luther King, Jr., Free at Last. David A. Adler (Holiday House)

Martin Luther King, Jr.: Leader in the Struggle for Civil Rights. Valerie Schloredt (Gareth Stevens)

Martin Luther King, Jr., and the March Toward Freedom. Rita Hakim (Millbrook)

Martin Luther King, Jr., Young Man With a Dream. Dharathula Millender (Macmillan)

Stride Toward Freedom. Reverend Martin Luther King, Jr. (HarperRow)

Where Do We Go From Here? Reverend Martin Luther King, Jr. (Beacon Press)

Videos

In Remembrance of Martin. (PBS)

Martin Luther King, Jr. (Schlessinger)

Martin Luther King, Jr.: From Montgomery to Memphis. (Phoenix/BFA)

Index